WOODY SHAW

JAZZ TRUMPET

Transcriptions from the Original Recordings

Transcribed by Dale Carley

Compilation by Eckart Rahn
Edited by Ronny S. Schiff

CELESTIAL HARMONIES, a division of MAYFLOWER MUSIC CORP., New York, New York

HAL•LEONARD® CORPORATION
7777 W. BLUEMOUND RD. P.O. BOX 13819 MILWAUKEE, WI 53213

DISCOGRAPHY

Title	Album/Label Number	Year
In A Capricornian Way	**Stepping Stones** • CBS AL 35560	*1978*
In Case You Haven't Heard	**Little Red's Fantasy** • MUSE 5103	*1978*
Katrina Ballerina	**The Moontrane** • MUSE 5058	*1975*
Little Red's Fantasy	**Little Red's Fantasy** • MUSE 5103	*1978*
The Organ Grinder	**Woody III** • CBS JC 35977	*1979*
Rahsaan's Run	**Rosewood** • CBS JC 35309	*1978*
Rosewood	**Rosewood** • CBS JC 35309	*1978*
Stepping Stone	**Stepping Stones** • CBS AL 35560	*1978*
Theme For Maxine	**Rosewood** • CBS JC 35309	*1978*
To Kill A Brick	**Woody III** • CBS JC 35977	*1979*
Tomorrow's Destiny	**Little Red's Fantasy** • MUSE 5103	*1978*
Woody I: On The New Ark	**Woody III** • CBS JC 35977	*1979*
Woody II: Other Paths	**Woody III** • CBS JC 35977	*1979*
Woody III: New Offerings	**Woody III** • CBS JC 35977	*1979*

Contents

In A Capricornian Way   **35**

In Case You Haven't Heard   **14**

Katrina Ballerina   **6**

Little Red's Fantasy   **10**

The Organ Grinder   **54**

Rahsaan's Run   **29**

Rosewood   **24**

Stepping Stone   **42**

Theme For Maxine   **32**

To Kill A Brick   **48**

Tomorrow's Destiny   **19**

Woody I: On The New Ark   **59**

Woody II:Other Paths   **64**

Woody III: New Offerings   **68**

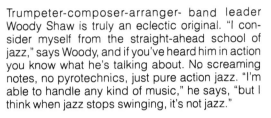

Trumpeter-composer-arranger- band leader Woody Shaw is truly an eclectic original. "I consider myself from the straight-ahead school of jazz," says Woody, and if you've heard him in action you know what he's talking about. No screaming notes, no pyrotechnics, just pure action jazz. "I'm able to handle any kind of music," he says, "but I think when jazz stops swinging, it's not jazz."

Shaw has demonstrated the ability to fit right in with the giants of every shade of the musical spectrum. The sound is his own, deeply personal, with a biting attack and an extraordinary gentle strength. The almost-bittersweet edge to his lyrical sound leaves listeners exceptionally moved.

Shaw says, "A complete jazz musician can play any style...(and) will love all phases of jazz music, not just one aspect." As all people, he is the sum total of his experiences. But it is significant that each learning experience gave him more tools to bring out his own individual talents. The more he absorbed, the wider his range of creativity and the stronger his identity.

The sum total of Shaw's experiences have been with the best. The musicians he's worked with, the musicians he's been influenced by are the trend setters, the innovators, the crème de la crème. Shaw is open and caring about giving these people credit for their influence on his style.

Woody's first musical experiences began with Jr. Elks and Jr. Masons Drum and Bugle Corps in Newark, New Jersey, playing bugle. Entrance into Cleveland Jr. High in Newark (at a time when there were still music programs in the Newark Schools turning out truly wonderful musicians the likes of: Wayne Shorter, Sarah Vaughan, Scott LaFaro and Betty Carter) brought Woody to the attention of one of the best trumpet teachers on the scene, Jerry Ziering. Ziering recognized the seriousness and the promise of Woody's talent and proceeded to give him the basis of a strong legit/classical background plus shaping his concept of jazz by bringing him solos by Dizzy Gillespie, Bix Biederbecke and Bunny Berigan.

Entrance to the Arts High School in Newark, playing in Ladozier Lamar's band at the Jones Street "Y" (the man responsible for heading Wayne Shorter, Walter Davis and Buddy Terry in the right musical directions) and gigging with the prestigious local bands of Brady Hodge, Nat Phipps and Allen Jackson brought Woody into contact with fine young musicians, many with already established reputations.

Woody's middle teens were a time of listening and "hanging out". Listening to idols Clifford Brown, Freddie Hubbard, Lee Morgan, Miles, meeting Benny Golson, Yusef Lateef and Betty Carter and getting pointers on everything from long tones to chords from Johnny Coles, Jimmy Anderson and Buddy Terry. With the recognition of Woody's talent came the invitations to sit in with established players at Len & Len's and Club 83 in Newark, first with Kenny Dorham and Hank Mobley plus a variety of known players: Johnny Griffin, Lou Donaldson, Stanley Turrentine, Jackie McLean.

Rufus Jones called Woody (at age 18) for his first road gig. Back in town he got his first big time gig with Willie Bobo in a club in Brooklyn. In the band at that time were Chick Corea, Larry Gales, Joe Farrell and Garnett Brown.

This was also the time that Avant Garde was making its mark, and the giant of the movement, Eric Dolphy, walked in and caught a set of Bobo's band and Woody. The next week he called Woody to join his band comprised of J. C. Moses, Bobby Hutcherson and Eddie Kahn. The Dolphy influence on Woody was profound. Woody states that, "Eric is the one who helped me find my own individual approach to playing trumpet."

Woody cut the albums, ERIC DOLPHY MEMORIAL and IRON MAN with Eric. Shortly thereafter Eric split with Mingus to Paris and eventually sent a ticket to Woody to join them. Ironically, as Woody was preparing to leave he heard Dolphy had mysteriously died. At everyone's urging Woody went to Paris, a place that gave him a chance to grow even more and work with Bud Powell, Kenny Clark, Art Taylor and Johnny Griffin.

After the Paris stint and a recording for MPS in Germany, Woody returned to the U.S. and joined Horace Silver's band (one of the three he always wanted to play with). Horace's band provided another one of those strong learning experiences for Woody absorbing from Horace more on form, structure, and discipline. With the addition of Tyrone Washington to the band, Horace felt that the strong force of Woody's and Tyrone's styles were affecting the band and they had to leave.

Then followed an incredible period with Woody working with the giants! Recording an album with Chick Corea, working and recording with Jackie McLean, McCoy Tyner, touring with Max Roach (number 2 of the 3 favorite bands), gigging with Clark Terry, forming a group with Joe Henderson and then joining Art Blakey and the Jazz Messengers (number 3 of the 3 favorite).

The early 70's found Woody on the West Coast, a weary and restless period, with gigs with Herbie Hancock and a group formed with Bobby Hutcherson. Woody credits Bobby with giving him a strong feel for the role of a good bandleader plus new directions in chords and style.

The turning point came in 1975. Woody recorded the MOONTRANE Lp for Muse. The strong rating in **down beat** plus excellent reviews everywhere underscored the reemergence of Woody and his increasing popularity.

Louis Hayes, Junior Cook and Woody put a band together in '75, but Woody continued gigging with other musicians, cut albums for Muse and LOVE DANCE became his first album on the charts. The quintet with Louis became the band Dexter Gordon used for his triumphant U.S. tour, his homecoming documented on the Lp HOMECOMING. Woody felt playing with Dexter was like playing with Trane or Bird...such a giant and legendary figure."

A wonderful lady came into Woody's life, Maxine Gregg, who became Woody's manager and wife. She's "Little Red" as in the title of Woody's Lp LITTLE RED'S FANTASY, the album where Woody, to quote Robert Palmer "...knew (there) was a territory he could stake out as his own and did it."

Then came ROSEWOOD, Woody's first album for Columbia and a long run on the charts, but nicest of all was the tribute of the *people* for ROSEWOOD was voted *Jazz Album of the Year* and Woody, *#1 Trumpet* in the down beat *1978 Readers Poll.*

ROSEWOOD was written for Woody's proud and supportive parents, "Rahsaan's Run" is Woody's tribute to Rahsaan Roland Kirk, "Theme for Maxine", written for Woody's wife and the whole album dedicated to Miles. The ever-caring, naturally responsive Woody.

It was Miles who had called Columbia and suggested they sign Woody. The instant success of ROSEWOOD followed by Woody's second Columbia Lp, STEPPING STONES proved Miles out and signaled that Woody had reached super-star status.

The album WOODY III shows just how innovative Woody is and as stated on Amiri Baraka's liner notes "…it's serious, aware of itself as an awareness of all that's gone before…and yet by its own existence affirming the promise and progress of the future." WOODY III notes the existence of the promise of the future in Woody Louis Armstrong Shaw, born in 1978, and those that have gone before Woody: Miles, Dolphy, Coltrane, Lee Morgan. Most of all, it shows integrity in music and it swings!

JAZZ TRUMPET SOLOS

Katrina Ballerina

Music by
WOODY SHAW

7

Little Red's Fantasy

Music by
WOODY SHAW

In Case You Haven't Heard

Music by
WOODY SHAW

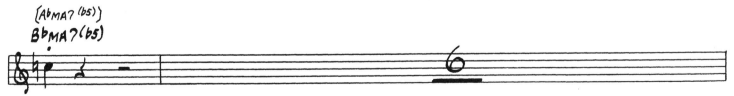

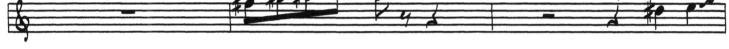

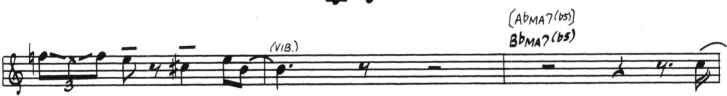

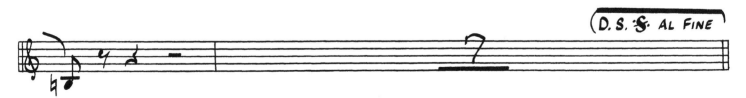

Tomorrow's Destiny

Music by
WOODY SHAW

Rosewood

Music by
WOODY SHAW

26

(V.S.)

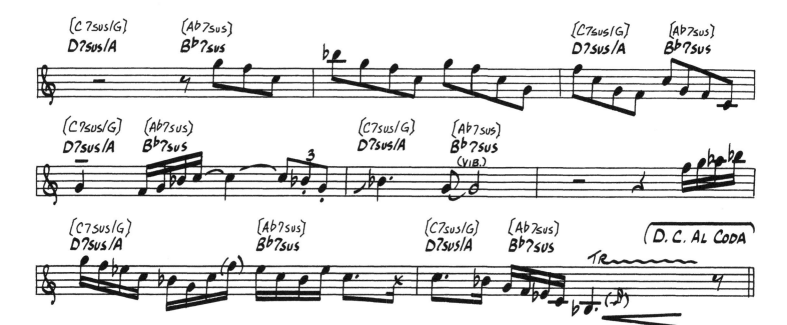

Rahsaan's Run

Music by
WOODY SHAW

Theme For Maxine

Music by
WOODY SHAW

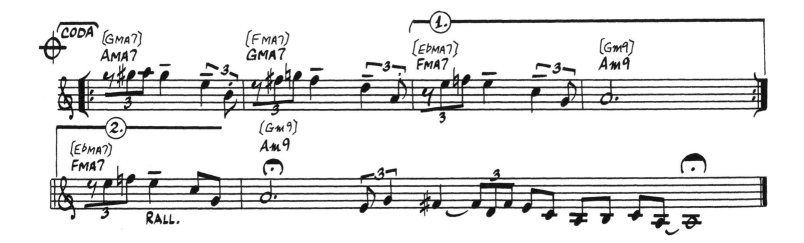

In A Capricornian Way

Music by
WOODY SHAW

40

Stepping Stone

Music by
WOODY SHAW

44

(TENOR SAX)

To Kill A Brick

Music by
WOODY SHAW

Fast Blues

52

The Organ Grinder

Music by
WOODY SHAW

58

Woody I: On The New Ark

Music by
WOODY SHAW

62

Woody II: Other Paths

Music by
WOODY SHAW

Woody III: New Offerings

Music by
WOODY SHAW